The Valley Press Anthology of Prose Poetry

edited by

ANNE CALDWELL &
OZ HARDWICK

Valley Press

and Northern Ireland. We were overwhelmed with submissions for this anthology and delighted by the quality of work, hailing from Shetland to the Isle of Wight, and from Northern Ireland to East Anglia. While it does not claim to offer a definitive survey, it nonetheless offers a snapshot of the best of contemporary writing in the form.

The writing is as diverse as the writers themselves, drawing on realism and surrealism, order and chaos, politics and play. We have tried to create a balance of new writers alongside more established voices, and we have allowed a wide variety of approaches to the form itself. Within our selection, it is possible to see the writing of a prose poem as close to musical improvisation, particularly jazz, where a musician might take an idea and explore just how far the musical phrase can be riffed or shaped. And, whether you read the collection sequentially or dip in at random, you will find that the individual pieces speak musically to each other in a surprising and dynamic conversation.

In the first issue of *The Prose Poem: An International Journal* (1992), Peter Johnson suggested that, 'Just as black humour straddles the fine line between comedy and tragedy, so the prose poem plants one foot in prose, the other in poetry, both heels resting precariously on banana peels.' Along with the emergence of digital literature and such genres as flash fiction, the hybridity, brevity, flexibility, and potential for surprise of prose poetry single it out as a form of writing that deserves recognition and further scholarly attention.

Participating in – and stimulated by – the International Prose Poetry Project instigated by the University of Canberra, we have both continued to develop our enthusiasm for the form. This project has initiated collaboration with over 30 international prose poets, sharing work on a weekly basis for the last five years, and has been instrumental in shaping our own research and editing project with Valley Press. Closer to home, we wish to thank Arts Council England who have supported us and recognised the need to raise the profile of prose poetry in the United Kingdom and beyond. Prose poetry provides a playful and condensed space for creative work to be shared, both in print and online, through smartphones, tablets and social media platforms. We are convinced that its creative possibilities will inspire the next generation of writers.

Prose poetry: a form that both combines and resists; a developing photograph; a hall of mirrors with the lights switched off; a Promethean form for unstable times.

Anne Caldwell and Oz Hardwick
For more information: prose-poetry.uk

Check-in

She lifted it from her handbag, placed it in the tray, gently, the way she'd set down a baby. The tip of the crescent gleamed, water-bright, but the surface was sky-bristled, chalk and old flour. The guard did not unfold his arms. *Is this electrical?* She shook her head. No – only a store of light, only the way a mirror holds your face inside. He touched the rim and she shuddered as if it was her own wrist. He traced its scythed edge with his fingertip. *A weapon?* She shook again, thinking of how it came to her, how she made her arms into a vase and let it slide the full chute of evening, land like an ice-skater recovering from a triple Lutz. How still it was in the end, how little like she imagined, brittle in chill weather, sweating in the daylight, how it shuddered on her windowsill, facing outside. Beside the scanner, the guards conferred. They sent the woman over in the end, the one who spoke gently when she gave the moon back to her. *You can't bring this through,* she said, *it's liquid, best drink as much as you can.*

Helen Mort

You Were Served Today By Janka

In transit we are all suggestible. It is this un-place causes us to order oysters. So when she mutters eyebrows, you stop. Yes, you'd like some. You have the time, and you have no eyebrows. You lost them, you tell her, as she settles you on the high stool. She peers, assessing. The eyebrows she has for you will be impermanent; won't wipe off when you sweat. (You sweat, you tell her, because of the side effects.) Her brush on your brow tickles. She has a tiny diamond in her front tooth. You see it after you close your eyes.

Claire Collison

Boat Party

The Thames is electric and the evening drunken; the lighting rig spinning pink and green out onto the river; every highlight on the water like a fag butt briefly sparkling then trod on, every ashy constellation lost in others. Below decks, it's hip-hop vs RnB and I think hip-hop is winning, just. We pass under Hungerford Bridge and for a few seconds worry that people will gob on our heads and in our pints, but then, in the space above a paddle steamer moored on the Embankment, the Houses of Parliament put their hands in the air, raise gun fingers to the sky, and some guy gives the finger to the building in general and shouts *fuck those pricks!* and we all laugh and repeat *fuck those pricks!* but I'm sure everyone is thinking of a different, individualised prick or set of pricks. We chug on into a Sex on the Beach-coloured sunset, and the moon is raw like a spot of flesh under peeled sunburn, and inside the crowd hammers on the low gilt ceiling as a track drops, and later there'll be ringing in ears and later there'll be strobes like lightning.

Natalie Whittaker

Gilese 876

All the absences have your face. I drink tea in their presence and think of you. I had to ask myself forgiveness for loving you, but I knew at once we had the same stars in the grit under our fingernails. I read horoscopes until the oil in my hands turned Aquarius to honey, then to amber. My mother stole that book in 1982, and I made Goodman's words into ants and they scurried into the sugar I lined up on the side like cocaine. We all have our fixations. Mother calls me unbalanced, but I laugh and say I still have both tits. We bonded about spending our childhoods wanting to hang ourselves so I guess she and I were right. There is no balance, and it is the same stars.

Kym Deyn

My mother is locked in a jar of ginger

I hear her battling with the lid, trying to hump herself out of the sickly liquid. It suits me not to let her out. I hear her invective – 'shite' and 'bugger'. I shall continue to disappoint. Her suspender is stuck; she is tugging at her roll-on. Let's have some music, something with a thump to it.

Linda Black

from *The Encyclopaedia of Forgotten Things*

When you hurl the paratrooper from your bedroom window, he hangs for a moment against the sun, making you screw up your eyes. His plastic backpack flips open, the red-white-blue silk billows in the air, and our childhoods linger, conscripted into a slow, slow freefall that matters so much we hold our synchronized breaths... until the crash on gravel – the disjointed figure lying in the yard, staring at the sky – and a silence in which we each expect the other to make some move to retrieve, to try again.

*

Every week, she has trudged the quarter mile to church, taken up her solitary bench, opened the hymn book, and done her best. But every week there is a new fluffed note or erroneous chord that adds to the catalogue of mistakes forgotten by everyone – except her. And today the archival muscle of her fingers has reached its limit. In the shuffling silence as the congregation prepares to draw breath, there's a cracking of joints, and an inexplicable click of her teeth like a malfunctioning machine, followed by nothing.

Paul Munden

Dress

The same uniform for twelve years. A white skirt, blue collar, blue belt, blue hem. A dark, no-nonsense kind of blue. White as snowfall in Eden. You washed it every single day, made sure you ate in small bites, always wore an extra pad so none of the blood could seep through. You began wearing that dress at the age of six, your skin haunted by the British flag, so you could be *Chinese with English characteristics*. Each time you wore it, you shut your body up. Some girls wore theirs short, discoloured, tight. As Head Girl, you reported them to the Office of the Headmistress for inappropriate behaviour, ignored their pleas, kept your own dress at just the right length.

Most mornings, you see the face of a boy in the mirror. You expect to fall in love with him, someday. Meanwhile, your fingers brush the wrist of another girl as you jostle into the assembly hall, and you understand that sin was never meant to be easy, only sweet. What memory might light up the pond you sat beside in dreams, eyeing so much depth it would be years before you dared? What curvature of tongue might you taste, as if another's breath were blessing? One night, you find yourself back there, kneeling beside the pond. You dream. A voice says: *Hell is not other people*. You slip into the water, stripped of the dress you wore for thousands of days.

Mary Jean Chan

Things that are tight

after Sei Shonagon

New elastic bands. The pages of a freshly bound book. Lids on jars of artichoke hearts. My heart. My neck. My smile. My spine. Things in my chest: dandelion buds that will never spore, ammonites, fists of fern, beetles, walnuts and pistachios I cannot crack, screwed up poems.

The bus driver's knuckles on the wheel as he swerves each time he coughs, skimming walls and cars and hedges. Suckling babies, piglets and puppies. Crossed legs. Crossed words. Fear.

Well-pitched tents. Well-strung washing lines. Well-tucked sheets. Tights. Buttons in button holes. Ruching. Jeggings. Cat suits. Leggings. Ballet shoes. Leotards. Oil in puddles. Corks. The breath in my lungs. Doors in frames. Cyclists in Lycra. Letters in envelopes. Bananas in their skins. Peas in a pod. Corn on the cob. Knives in the knife block. The pith and peel of lemons.

Kith and kin. Blood ties. Blood clots. Fish scales. Bats' wings. Motets. Knitted scarves. Napkins bound by napkin rings. Wedding rings. Engagement rings. Eternity rings. The muzzle on a Rottweiler. Handcuffs. Padlocks. Rhinestone studs in an ear. Braces. A string of pearls. The song of a sky lark. Waterfalls. Girdles. Crabs in their shells. Fake greetings. Insincere smiles. Ice skating boots. Newly-weds. Wine in the rack.

Well-told lies. The dove-tailed trill of starlings. Limpets. Locks. Passwords.

Storm clouds before they split. Eggs before they hatch. Leeches.

The stripes on a zebra. Musical manuscripts. An orchestral suite. A crowded lift going down and down and down below the ground floor. Passport control. Sardines in a tin. The front of his knees tucked into the back of my knees as we sleep. Sugar lumps.

Gaia Holmes

Twelve Dark Passages No.6

Having established a bedrock of pure darkness we may perhaps be able to name its sub-classes, all the classic blacks we know. Let's say their names: *Ebony, Taupe, Davy's Grey, Noir, Charcoal, Soot, Jet, Onyx, Lamp Black, Carbon Black, Super Black, Vantablack. That black.*

The black of your polished shoe, the black of the ribbon on the undertaker's hat, the black of drypoint in curled metal. The raven, the crow, the rook, the blackbird, the black swan. And other blacks. Keep adding. These are only names, and names are there to be invented. But do it in darkness. In the dark backward and abysm of time. In time's eloquence. In time's infinite capacity and its vast belly that keeps expanding and never will stop expanding.

Are we there yet? Is the thought of time a black thought yet? Is darkness visible supposed to be visible?

It's just a room. These are just thoughts waking to find themselves returning as words. But they are waking in darkness, a darkness in which it makes no difference whether your eyes are shut or not.

George Szirtes

Apples on a Tree

Yesterday as we sat out over lunch you were facing the delphiniums and plums and I was looking towards the apple tree, laden with perfect ripening fruit now, whereas last year the apples were few and, though edible, discoloured and blemished. We discussed in a kind of counterpoint the glory of apples and apple-trees, you tending towards praising the harvest we would have from them, and urging me not to get rid of the folded cardboard packing-cases in the garage, we'd need them to spread on the floor of the stable block, where the swallows nest every summer in the gloom, and lay out the ripe apples in long rows; me keeping on about how I loved them as a spectacle now, with all their promise, not as big as they will be but huge in my sight, having watched them grow, and found them after days away or busy to have leapfrogged stages like grandchildren. This rainy morning, moving about in the gloomy kitchen, I glanced through glass and saw them, still round and perfect, gleaming even in subdued light. Yesterday I had a revelation that being almost perfectly spherical and glossy-skinned they reflected sun no matter what angle it was shining from. They are sources of folklore, folksongs, crumble, pies, cider and juice, and memories of sugary casings that threatened teeth. And reflections of our life here, together, like a hearth, an axletree.

John Freeman

High Tide at the Spit

There must be a name for the moment of change. When confusion, however beautiful, Leaves us, and regular, longshore waves fold themselves at our feet.

At last glance we were all frolics and swells, outright playful splashes. White foam skipping boundaries. Ripples widening like batter right to the edges of the pan.

Before that: glass stillness, whitetops, diamond makings and breakings, point of intersection delineating a straight line along underlying sand.

And in the beginning: two sides of a triangular bit of land, little peninsula sunk in jade green. How fast will water come in? Are those fish? How long will this last?

Life tends toward the universal: wind and gravity and the changing shape of the shore means waves travel the same direction eventually, at the same speed, in the same general fashion.

Whatever, you understand, may lie beneath.

Patricia Debney

My Mother, the Monsoon

I go out early to do her messages, to avoid her Brylcreemed exes who will dip in at the bookies, betting on snow for Christmas, rain on St Swithin's Day. And her brigade of lady-friends who breakfast, who finger meaty garnets at their throats and linger over each other's wrinkles, ogling. The comedy of correctness. Back home, the house is full of ticks; of mad cousins making money, breaking culture with karate chops, gnawing on it with their eyeteeth. Moderation is one over the top for the mother. Who is family for the old lady dwindling, circled by doctors and district nurses like the farmer's wife in her den? The beautiful and the stunned. I'm suddenly dumped into a whole year of mouldy Mondays, arcane and off the boil. Be still for the postman, lick his lovely thumb. Dumb-lovely, plump with packages. If you are good he will give you a neighbour's missive. It's not considered dishonest any more, he says, he has a dispensation and is probably double-jointed. This family is a becalmed army, idiot with sealed passion. Mother has climate change for a personality. I have become one of the draughts in a stately home, brocade-curtained and visited nostalgically. Don't take me for lost. I have cleaned the carpet of every room with my rasping tongue, rinsed each with tears. Don't take me for the host. Be sick, she says, it's less risky and you'd make a lovely corpse, chisel-cheeked, and modest. She rains for half my life.

Geraldine Clarkson

Mowing

I cannot write about mowing the lawn while I mow it. I cannot write on the white brick wall, or on the back of my other arm. I cannot write on anything in the garden while I struggle with the orange cord that keeps wrapping around my boot and throwing itself in the mower's path. I cannot write about mowing while I mow, about the rhythm of the blades over the deep field of grass, about the growl and shear as they slice stones and muddy earth. I cannot write about the cold breeze on the back of my neck as I work over the same ground three times, the lawn calf-deep and soaked from autumn rain. While I mow, I cannot write about the grassy tang that smells of *haricot vert,* green beans. I cannot write about mowing as I move the orange metal from corner to corner, tree to tree, the pavement mapping the shape of lawn grown wild. I cannot write it as I wrestle with the beast this lawn has become after months of not mowing. I can't mow when I must write, so I make the whirring stop, then crouch to collect mounds of grass too wet to be sucked into the mechanism: mossy with leaf mulch, trampled by the mower's triple pass. I clear them to clear my head. I gather the clumps until my hands are green with crushed chlorophyll, until my fingertips are gold with new words and the light of grass on my skin.

Liz Bahs

The Tales

*

The maid stood at the edge of the city and opened the cage of her chest. Her heart preened its wings of arterial blood and then flew. Up it went, high, high as the cathedral spire. She returned to the palace and made beds, tight as drums.

*

One morning, when the cloak-maker had finished a long night of stitching, his fingers aching, the fabric spotted with his own blood, he sat in the stillness and observed his labours. Even the sun was not stout enough to penetrate the deep valleys of the cloak.

*

What use is a head? thought the gardener as he scythed off his own and those of his groundsmen. The heads rolled into the palace's ha-ha. Bees were occupied like any other day. A mole mined a path under the neat rolled lawn.

Helen Ivory

After the Accident

Somewhere in England – Norfolk, maybe – there are birds which imitate mechanical sounds. Car alarms; mobile ringtones; sirens. Sirens. In a white, urgent rectangle bleeding loud light onto the pavement, the girl arrived here. Maybe birds, unreal in the red glow, sang their urban songs to each other beneath the sound.

She wouldn't know.

Her body is learning to speak the language of machines. Sign language first: green, bright fingers retracting and releasing like claws, like tape measures. When they overreach, the body sings with mechanical urgency, increasing speed. Sound is carried along wire vocal cords from the tiny pinprick mouths on her hands and in the damp space of her fossa.

In Berlin, nightingales have learned to cry louder than the traffic. The girl on the bed has not been to Berlin (and it is likely now that she never will) but she is competing to be heard. Whisper, speak, scream – until blue buttons and clean hands silence her. Gentle pressure. And a sharp scratch.

Becky Balfourth

Nightcombing

The sea dozes, lulled by its own monotony. She pries shells from the hearts of hagstones, plenty of salty gristle at every tug and pluck. Out there where the sea is taller than thirty men, red lights flash. A coven of boats gathers at the cauldron's rim under the sign of the inverted plough, Orion on his head, belt adrift. Both of these are correct. Her feet have walked for miles on the same tilting square of sand, watch-hands turning like a crazed compass. She's late, she's late for every important date. *Come walk through my clefty shadows* says the cliff in the voice of an aunt she never knew. The moonlight on her skin turns her face to mould.

Sue Burge

Purple

1.

Purple capes me in womanhood, like the maxi-coat I bought, aged eighteen. It gave me buttons to open, one by one, watched by another in my tiny bedsitter. Purple pressed me, girl to woman.

2.

A purple orchid grows in the grass, next to my head. My legs spread, spliced for you. Inspiration, no doubt, for purple prose when you dip your nib in ink for literary purposes, when we are finished. Your book will sell well, and I will cry, hidden by purple drapes – safety curtain of the theatre.

3.

Purple tunics, shoes, sheets and pillows, all threaded through with blues and patched with reds. Happy purple, plaintive purple, perhaps purple, depending on the day, the night. Today, purple thins to mauve.

Ceinwen E. Cariad Haydon

Hellbox

My mother had two mouths. One was for saying. The other was for not saying. She kept a budgerigar padlocked in a tarnished cage in the attic. At dusk she would climb to the top of the house with a lime green feather boa on her bony resurrected shoulders. She would sing to the bird and watch its confusion. Later, she would preen it with her bird-cat tongue. She would tell it: *Listen, can't you? After all this, someone, somewhere still calls out to me in prayer.*

Heidi Williamson

Hellbox: where 'bad' characters go: a receptacle for broken and battered letters.

Desolation

a small town   a long way from anywhere   the only road out is
so little used that it is hard to find   there is a river   of course
there is a river   it flows tears across the rocks   tumbling forever
in a silent force   and new life   there is none   just scenes from
old movies   some shot in sepia   fixed in a loop   to run forever
and a day   it is hard to tell who gets things done in Desolation
the barman is always busy   serving only shots and the occasional
glass of red wine for the more refined mourner of hope   the
writers line the bar of course   the loudest and most awkward
being the poets   closely followed by the journalists with their
similar need to dissect and expose but with less of the direct line
to the killing phrase   somewhere in the shadows lurks a painter
or two and the sculptors   the musicians have their own clique
and cliques within cliques   the comedians have their own
version of hell somewhere over the hills that no one cares to visit
real cigarettes are still smoked here   they are the only currency
except for longing looks and pallid attempts at seduction   which
fool no one

Nick Allen

It's about a boy

When he came over that time just to see me and not the others, who I think were at the cinema, I thought I had succeeded. So, as my head began to fill as it always does when I see him, he told me he wasn't sure how to feel. And when my head was 1/6 full I told him I wasn't the best person to ask because I was lost and I wasn't going to find myself here. And at 1/5 he told me that that didn't matter and he wanted me to choose. Selfish. A quarter up I said I was elsewhere and to come back another time. 1/3 and he touched my hand to remind me that I was lying. Half way full I said I needed to lie down and so he lifted my eyes with his and he held my lungs in each hand as we walked to the floor together. And when my head was close to full he said I was everything he had never wanted. That's why it hurt so much when he left, because my head was so full so I couldn't tell him he was nothing I had ever needed and that's why we were meant to be lying on that floor together. Because we made sense of each other's confusion.

Ailish Fowler

The Rooms Behind the Eyes

"There is the sun dissolving the dark, and light as clear as music, filling the room where you sleep and the other rooms behind your eyes."
— *Jeanette Winterson*

I want to be still – So still that air sleeps on my skin and the tick of a watch could rattle my bones. I will put my name and number in an envelope and post it to the moon, apply no pressure to my surroundings or the floor. I have no need for ornament or embellishment, clothes or colours applied to my surfaces. I am a hairless shape. I want to be carried by time, my breathing to fade, my heart to suspend its beat and my pale eyes to make one last slow blink like the shutter of a camera without film. And from that instant I have no smell and my impossibly smooth surface is neither wet nor dry, my inside and outside will irreversibly merge. All natural colours have drained so I become transparent and, eventually, will posses neither length, width nor depth. What has happened has been made possible by a wish and can never be repeated or forgotten and what is left of me is a nothingness that is bigger and more powerful than time or you or me. It can never be destroyed or remoulded and there is no box large enough for it to live in – There is no hum of electricity.

Winston Plowes

I Cook Welsh

I am cutting up meat on my counter top calling to my motherhooded ghosts who cured pork in hot blue smoke and kept ice to grind. Granny E melted chicken on trivets for all the times rain slanted down the door – in Wales every day. Black gold and slate and rock cakes and rock pasties and rock falls. Have any ancestors o' mine o' mine slit a pig's throat and undressed birds to pimpled skin? People and the pits. I sing-song as I rub in salt, pepper, hot red paprika. I have killed snails and spiders and I did not eat their strange anatomy, o' mothers o 'mothers.

A spear shaft in my hand. Whip of bow string. Mud making home in my angles. Running free. I bite my tongue to taste wildblood, tripping on the echo-field of prehistory by my kitchen sink. Rub in garlic, mustard and all your desire and eat it juicy, with sharp onions, with bare hands.

Haley Jenkins

Ghetto van Gogh

The night my mother tells the story of the thief, I am cross-legged on her lap. Her mouth is inches from my ear. She lets dusk slip into her voice and whispers about the boy who snatched a mango at the market and ran, becoming the teenager who robbed a shop at gun point, shot the blind cashier, shot him as he fell, shot him once more dead; became the man who stole 36 cars and when apprehended, to be publicly hanged, asked for one wish, his whole lip quivering.

My mother, who is inches from my ear, explains his dying wish to speak to his mother. The silent crowd parted, she gathered his bound wrists to her lips, kissed his rough skin, her cheeks shimmering in the killing heat. He bent forward, my mother says, her mouth even closer, her dusky voice hushed, bent forward as if to kiss her cheek goodbye and switched sharply, bit into her ear, strained against the flesh, ripped the thing off and spat you should have told me, mother, what I did was wrong.

Inua Ellams

Bread, orange, aura

She went to a camp where the coach was so angry she didn't feed them breakfast, or the coach was so angry she made a pot of tea and a bowl of bread and put them in the middle of the table, and they were scared of her, so didn't touch anything. She went to a school where they exercised in the morning before lessons. They would stand in a field in rows and stretch their fingers and their necks. Their backs would be stretched on Wednesdays. They all wore orange tracksuits. Some mornings the fog would be so thick that it cut people in half and fifty-one percent of the world would go missing. Sometimes she would be put in touch with distant relatives who didn't respond to her earnest emails. Sometimes she would challenge herself to not eat lunch, especially when the coach had refused to give them breakfast. She went to a school where ten percent of her marks were based on her aura. Her aura was the feeling of returning to primary school and being too big for the chairs. Some weekends she went home on the train with her friends. They hunched over their phones trying to complete calculations the fastest, talked about what the bread would taste like if they dared.

Jenna Clake

Forget the Humans

up there making underwater motions: what about, say, their rivets?
holding everything together unmoving, looking no matter what
like the ideal of themselves, and, better, unthinking – meaning
afterwards the earth's gravity won't crush them like a glorious
childhood.

Kristian Doyle

Solo

Fingers like hers miss the smoking carriage, restless with a rolled ticket. In other circumstances they could have played – guitar? piano? cello, even? – but they were born to the wrong body, hobbled by the same spike of chance that does what it will with us all. Every day she gets off at the factory, comes back in the evening unchanged. I don't know what they do there, but it dries out hands, draws skin tight under eyes, drapes the day's heaviness around puffa-jacketed shoulders. No-one that age doesn't have a phone except her, and she looks at – not through – the window with an expression that says *I am a long way from my world, but my eyes have not forgotten soft hills and honey-coloured stone, the accent of a swinging gate, the promise upon promise of a river that flows from my grandmother's cupped hands.* She has never smoked, but her fingers roll the ticket, roll everything tight, itching to set it all alight.

Oz Hardwick

Signal on

My mother is watching *The Fall of the House of Usher* in the living room, which shares a wall with the room where I was born. This is, perhaps, one of my first solid memories. One of hers, recounted many times, is the one about grandparents who moved to Gluehouse Lane to get a council house. *Stay there for three months and you'll be made*, someone said. A way from the town, and not far from the Tyne, she walks into the scullery at midnight. The crick-crack underfoot, her arches pricking on the floor as it skews and skitters, a new smell in the air. Standing still, then she retreats, trying to put her feet back into steps she's made. Up on tiptoes she flicks the Bakelite switch. At first, it's not obvious what she's looking at, then it begins to make some kind of sense. She had heard stories but had never – until then – seen so many cockroaches in such a small space, every inch of floor covered; on the inside of the step, round the benchtop edges, lining the skirting edge. And as the light comes on, the slick unzips down the middle, revealing the grey pocked lino beneath. She focuses on one that falls

Lisa Matthews

once more

everything comes from it and returns to it

even elastic bands breathe slowly in and out feign sleep feign like
a bat hung on dusk she listens to his breathing in and out of what
she longs for the letters of her name *unzipping once more* even
elastic bands dissect are slower than paper than he lets slip the
dark once more she lies *on he and she* touching her waiting beside
him once more ropes of the night very slowly the ropes of night
tighten once more beside her the man *lies the man beside her lies*
the silence *lies she* was she the silence even elastic bands yearn
the sheets between he and her conceal the man sinks his chin
sinks the silence in the pillow and further beyond his breathing
forehead his jaw his body falls once more about what his dream
not ask falls his dream once more she reads blackberry bushes
on the ceiling once more once more her breath searching for his
buttocks his back his hand once more she may she once more?
Turn around you turn around.

Astrid Alben

The Manual of Proper Lawn Care

All summer you've reminded me of a bad back winter, that December when I was four. My father pulled something and each night, barefoot, I'd walk along his spine. He said it was the only time nothing hurt.

You walk just like that. Careful sharp footsteps, spikes on the soles of your shoes. It's because the lawn's dying. *The Manual of Proper Lawn Care* tells us to *aerate the ground, sow seeds, feed,* yet yellow patches appear. Some of it looks like it's been on fire.

The children we never had started arriving at Christmas. Occasionally, we'd spot one peering at the tree, nose to the window, leaving breath smudges like a knuckleduster. We never let them inside. Now, they run wild.

The boys leave daily birds' nests on our doorstep. I search but never find which tree they came from. They hate me for trying and start smashing eggs.

You step over the shells with the lawn sprinkler. Five fresh black patches appeared in the night. It's because of the girls

They're different to boys. Quieter. They pick flowers and fritter the petals into pots to make perfume. When the rosewater grows furry with mould, they tip out their failures and start fires.

One kid looks just like you. She frowns at her fingers and pours her bottle of nail polish out on the ground. Her sisters gather, staring at the puddle like a pearl that's given up the will to be strapped around a neck. Giggling, they paint all the flowers with nail polish, then someone strikes a match. They may stink at perfume, but they've got this down to a fine art.

The roses glow, holding their shape for a surprisingly long time before they fall to ash. It's beautiful, other than the fear the whole place will burn down. It makes me feel stupid for ever putting roses in a vase. They burn like sunsets that make you rush for a camera but aren't supposed to catch.

I stand under the pagoda pointing to the flickering lawn. Girls lighting fires, boys flinging arrows, piss everywhere.

You lean on your rake and look over the garden. You see nothing but one baby asleep under the lilacs, another lace cradle swaying in the breeze.

Angela Readman

The Coffin Calendars

Miss June is given lilies, Miss
December's in white fur. In the
woods, twelve walnut caskets
for us to stand in. Childhood
Sundays, the moth-eyed rows of
old men, half-living. *Memento mori*
paintings hanging on the walls, the
angels in the aisles with noseless
shadows. My smile says too much
about my skull. I try to stay still
– the photographer says next year
we'll all have guns and camouflage
bikinis. In town, people turn
their heads as far as owls do. Our
dresses show the winged blades of
our backs as we fly off the shelves
– and the men, the men joke they
can't see the coffins.

Charlotte Eichler

The House that Jack Built

I entered the museum that contained the house that Jack built. The original purpose of the house had been to keep everyone out, and I thought the game would be to find the secret door. I found instead a house without walls. A man with a strong, kind face was cooking broth on a stove for two boys in nightshirts, who had fallen asleep over a kitchen table. The scene looked warm and welcoming, yet I felt increasingly irritated by a faint waxen glow surrounding it. Moreover, ever since entering the museum I'd had the distinct sensation that the fingertips of my right hand were brushing against the bottom of someone's front teeth. I decided to have a word with the museum attendant.

Ian Seed

Running, I become

three bridges – over the old red sandstone bridge, under the concrete bridge, speeding up to reach the arches of the Royal Border Bridge; the piers above me, an open-air cathedral. I become a woman running with water and mudflats, with North Sea and estuary, drawing towards the river's source. Running minus earphones, I become music, passing through *Melancholy*, where the shorelarks' warbling slows down. I become November, gloveless hands, face chilling to painless, oil of clove dissolving. Running, I become the woman with ten-metre legs, with a pinhead – contents so scanty it no longer needs to survey the horizon for obstructions. I become significant to dogs, who bark to run with me, whose owners now address me – 'Did you just pass a man with a big black dog?' No breath to explain that her three ankle-hungry Jack Russells worry me more than one giant lollopy dog. Running, redrafting myself, I return to my primal language of sigh and puff and laugh; I become sweat and tear, the low-thud song of my lungs. Running, I become a woman wintering; I follow the pink-footed geese crossing the hard blue sky in a great wavering *W*, and when it sharpens to a *V*, a letter of purpose, I join the formation of those who know where to go and how and why, gliding upstream in their upwash, their wingbeat. Running, I become the border.

Anne Ryland

Carpenter

Imagine a carpenter who does
not know their tools, how join
meets join and together make
a frame that supports a whole.
When asked how dowel or mitre
get their strength, they don't
point at joints and shrug, say
*I've no idea, I just like to work
with wood.* The dovetail, cross
lap, tongue & groove; mastered
by the hours of craft, of graft,
toil & sweat, of finger joint or
dado, birdsmouth, or cross lap,
a floating tenon; stitch & glue
with copper wire, resin, an eye
for the specifics holding up
your house, your home, the digs
in which you rest a head after
sharing all the words you say
you love, but do not know a tool
is useful in the crafting of a
line. You write? Remember this:
Learn to justify, break a page,
learn what should be centred.

Robert Harper

A New Career in a New Town

David Bowie called. Before I could get into the specifics of him being dead and this being a private, unlisted number, he said, 'That's a foreign ring-tone, man – are you abroad? Always had you pegged as a bit of a stop-at-home, curled up in your Yorkshire foxhole.' I told him I was in Ysp, flirting with communism, alienation and Class A narcotics, and working on my experimental Ysp trilogy. He said, 'Simon, your imagination is telling lies in the witness box of your heart. But listen, will you write the lyrics for my next album?' 'Why not,' I replied, and quickly we thrashed out a plan of action. It would all be done by electronic communication – no personal contact, no face-to-face meetings. David *laid down some backing tracks* and over the next year or so I worked up a suite of songs – verse-chorus stuff, nothing too pretentious or avant-garde. 'These are genius, man. You could have been a poet!' he said, laughing like a cheeky cockney in the saloon bar of a south London boozer circa 1969, his voice like cigarette smoke blowing through a pre-loved clarinet. 'One thing I always wanted to tell you, David,' I said. 'When I was about thirteen, I was really into table tennis but had no one to play with. It was just me versus the living room wall, on the dining room table. One night I went down to the local youth club, where all the roughnecks used to hang around, and made my way to the top floor where the roughnecks were playing table tennis, lads who'd stolen cars and thrown punches at officers of the law. I was wearing shorts and sweatbands in the style of my favourite Scandinavian table tennis champion of the era whose deceptive looping serve I hoped one day to emulate and whose life I wanted to live. I felt like a kid goat pushed into the tiger enclosure at feeding time, but they ignored me, those roughnecks with their borstal-spot tattoos and broken teeth, just carried on playing, the small hard electron of the ball pinging back and forth across the net like the white dot in that seventies video game.' 'Pong,' said David. 'Exactly,'

I said, 'Just carried on smoking and swearing and hammering the ball to and fro under the yellow thatch of the canopied light in the darkened upstairs room. And here's the thing: every time he hit a winner, the roughest of those roughnecks would sing a line from *Sound and Vision*. "Blue, blue, electric blue, that's the colour of my room," he'd croon as he crashed a forehand to the far corner of the table, or "Pale blinds drawn all day," when he flipped a cheeky backhand top-spinner past his bamboozled opponent. You probably scribbled those words on a coaster in a Berlin cocktail bar or doodled them with eye-liner pencil on a groupie's buttock, but they'd carried all the way to a dingy youth club in a disused mill under a soggy moor, into the mouth of one of those roughnecks, who's probably dead now or serving life.' David sounded pensive on the other end of the phone, perhaps even a little tearful. 'I have to go now,' he said. I could hear the technician checking his seatbelt and oxygen line for the last time, touching up his mascara, lowering his visor. Then the engines started to blast and the countdown began. I wandered down to the big Henry Moore in the park and lay on my back in the crook of its cold bronze curve, watching the skies, waiting for the crematorium of night to open its vast doors and the congregation of stars to take their places and the ceremony to begin.

Simon Armitage

Conversations in the Cornfield

Angel in the cornfield, better than any scarecrow. six wings, six eyes, six limbs. the number of the Angel is sixsixsix and they only ever answer if you say it thrice in latin. Latin is a dead language. Angels are a dead concept. i used to think corn was golden until i saw the Angel's wings. then i realised that human perception misses out on all sorts of colours. we're limited that way. sometimes i whisper old prayers. our father who art in heaven. my father who is not god but still taught me that to turn to a pillar of salt would be a blessing. morning breaks bloody and bruised. the Angel stands in the cornfield. a rotten tooth in the mouth of the world. the broken glass in the gutter. swept away during morning clean up with the rest of last night's bad decisions. i saved a lizard from the train tracks yesterday. it was tiny and easily missed. the Angel is bigger than the lizard. i don't know how to move them off the train tracks. i don't ask them about heaven or salvation or forgiveness. instead i tell them about how i'm bad at practising the piano and that i went to catholic school to get away from old bullies and instead found new, worse bullies and how i saw a video on making your own kombucha and how it felt the first time i kissed a girl. the Angel tells me my progress forward might cost me those who wish me to be static. i joke that the TV has only been static since they arrived because i'm uncomfortable with the thought of abandonment even if i'm not the one being abandoned. the Angel tells me there's never anything good on TV these days anyway.

K. Blair

Wild Garlic and Detours

Alice can sense them all, pulling away from shadows of their loved ones, late in the evening when everything cools and lengthens and light catches the beech leaves.

The dead are walking backwards, skirting through the woods towards the Calder River and Crimsworth's deep ravine, murmuring to each other. Some are lingering near the water; some are climbing up through the banks of wild garlic, some gather bluebells to remind themselves of the living, to remind themselves that summer's nearly here and soon the meadowsweet will drown them all in scent.

Anne Caldwell

|∧∧∧*

when we can no longer take the amount of blood on the walls
stairs and carpets on the windows and mirrors in the cups and
saucers on the plates and forks and spoons and knives when we
can no longer accept the amount of blood sold in the marketplace
when we can no longer agree to the amount of blood discussed at
committee meetings when we can no longer drink another drop
of blood despite the landlord taking our car keys when we can
no longer bear the weight of blood on the roof in our pockets
pulling at our belts filling the scratches tumbling about our heads
coursing through the fields and rivers lying heavy like a cloud
low above the city when we can no longer wipe this blood from
our brows and fingers when we can take no more blood no more
bleeding when we can take no when we blood when blood when
blood blood blood when the blood when blood when we can
mount the blood no longer when the blood is blood nothing but
its own blood nothing but blood

Mark Russell

Picture of the Dead Woman as a Bride

She's so thin – hitched to the left, snapped in the middle like a broken stick. As if she's saying, *I'm sorry. Sorry for being so tall.* It's the seventies, so her dress is a mix of peasant-milkmaid, Victorian high-buttoned neck and frill. Her hair is acorn brown, swooped to the side with lacquer. Her face is scrubbed. She is cradling pink roses as they bud from a mist of baby's breath. Her clutch on the spray is rigid, veins spindling the back of her hand. Her elbow-length veil is fixed to her head with a band of satin flowers – it's too much round her face. It nets her in. Later, three children will add to her girth but for now, a pearly clasp rides the small circumference of her waist. Her chest looks hollow, scooped as the breeze drifts through her satin snow. Thirty eight years later, she killed herself. I know that I am searching her body for clues, trying to measure her eyes for reasons why. I put my palm over half of the photograph, blank out the man so I see only her. She is untethered, floats from the portrait. A rising cloud.

Jane Burn

Letter from Terry

And so to be able to perform nothing you need to provide the audience with a simple reading, Terry writes. Drama without drama, complication or crisis. It should be a no-performance, long enough (although how long is long enough you may rightly wonder, or more precisely how short is short enough to avoid lapsing, hurting, harming within the short time we have before we die) so people can come and go until they get bored or tired or simply aware of time. The weave of language and content has to be its own thing, no sense in decoration. The cut and paste of the unexpected echoes, the random, unfitting pieces will weave a fit architecture, a fabulous journey for the voice, our testimony of *no*. It is like my own deviant path to learning about the world – acknowledgedly partial and fragmented and infinite. And so, see, your empty swimming pool, your precious pool *sans* pool, *sans* water, like the no text, that which still remains a text with texture, made of living fabric, is textured of binaries, a kind of building that inherently carries, or I should say quietly confronts unbuilding within itself. This private inner conflict is what produces *nothing, our* inner no, because, needless to say, we must take care of it, in other words, we must feel *something*, in other words, one must care. No means no, that's right but our prohibitions, the bans and bars in and on our lives, chosen or given, do, with time, morph into affection. And so, vice versa, our deepest intimacy into obstinacy and so tight-lipped silence. But there is always hope for love. Hope is the last to go. I have no doubt. A yes to life is no to death. A yes to death is a no to life. A no to life is a yes to death. A yes to death is a no to life. A no to death is a no to life. A yes to death is a yes to life. The syllogism is open, endless, infinite, if you like. And so, since you have asked, we will perform nothing as something in disguise masking it as everything in disguise of nothing, made of and in this world, a world that's partly and wholly part of the other world, constituted from nothing, our non-being, our no-thing, as partially and wholly part of something, a paradox your own sadness is made of, like the parable of the loathing lover, long gone, still inhabiting you, or the permutation of the phantom swimmer dormant, idle, still still in the real swimmer, the carcass of the dead typist in the (also already) dying author, the poet in absentia, who does not exist, still set still in lotus pose at the margin of the poem that exists, your most precious thing, or like our own alter ego always already in incognito, the way you too mute from the mutability of you, or let alone the poem, the total tautologiser, composed from the same and only poem, that is, of nothing else other than itself, so does nothing permeate from nothing, as your pool from the many inner pools, permeates from something, and being constituted of something, a living thing, like the pool, or the poem, or the paradox of sadness in you, it is made of our own emptiness, it's made of us. So bon courage. And she signs off with *love, Tiresias.*

Ágnes Lehóczky

Cups

A storm is coming. The forecasters warn of gales to rival '87. Inside the café though, Claire sees nothing but calm. Racks of fine china line the far wall, teacups dangle from hooks, a series of orderly rows from worktop to ceiling. When tea is poured it remains polite and brews just as it always has. Cups still fit their saucers, the rattle of held crockery as familiar as an elderly relative. In three years of Wednesday evenings, even the little things have failed to change. It's time she moved on, people keep saying.

In the group, one woman talks of Ray – how it started about this time last year; how winter draws in, drags the darkness closer from the edges; how their community is teeming with strugglers and wobblers, they just don't get given a microphone often; how this is a time to remember the damaged, and shun the slick slogan: "Hard-working people who want to get on." Get on to *where*?

The woman chokes up, waits fifteen seconds. The silence grows around her; then she offers her poem, describing the ground as it rushed towards her friend. Claire wants to stand up and tell her it's true: however far we climb, the hard ground is always there waiting to greet us. But her throat sticks, she stares at the wall. These are the moments she fears to remember. If the storm were to blow through the door of this shop, only gravity would try to keep the cups in their places.

Michael Loveday

Reef

(On the use of coral-based bone implants)

It is the year I dream of fish. Not cetaceans. Tiny masked fish nibble at my eyelashes, their beaks inlaid with emerald. Parrotfish and jewelled wrasse, drunk on salt, weave among the swaying follicles of my hair. On the third day, scarlet seeds burrow into the pith of my skull, their shy fronds uncurl.

The second year, they X-ray me: screw deeper into the marrow. Seas pour in, circulate my head until the brain is sponge. A bone-locked ocean booms. Words dissolve: vowels snag on teeth, consonants wash from my tongue.

By the last year, we are many; dendritic, memory grafted from pillar to branch. This is our colony: a splotched colossus rooted in cortex spreading to stem. Pronouns bleach from maps, coastlines fade. Coordinates stain like ego.

Susie Campbell

Fruit

It took fifteenyears to realise that the lasteveningsun fell on the shed, to pull it down, and now to sit-here, thinking of all the other things which take a longtime to learn, like silence and rest; to look at the Arum lilies holding their improbably whitetrumpets to the sun and remember it took them fifteenyears to settle into their newhome, grieving for my childhoodgarden, for that particular fall-of-light, for the voice-and-step of the one who used to tend them; thinking of allthethings I'll never learn, like mandarin, icedancing, saxophone, and all the things I can't-make-right, the enormity of knowing; watching the lemontree, with its white, waxy flowers, slowly learning to be fruit.

Maggie Butt

The Gewgaw Man

HE'S OUT there. Right outside the whitewashed walls of our cottages of sorrow.

Sometimes he lies low, making noises in the night – random yelps and yowls that overcharge our jumpy hearts.

Sometimes he slips round to flimsy back doors and rat-tats on the glass with a grin. Every time a different face revealed then reclaimed by the dark.

Other times he's brazen, parading up and down, clothed in gold: a one-man big brand show. Making us look, making us ache, filling us up with clouded longing.

It's a scandal, what he's doing to us.

Replacing the fire in our veins with tissue paper flames; laying traps on the routes that lead out of this town – to places we now only hazily recall.

It's no good going to the Neighbourhood Watch – he's given them all new iPhones.

We'd ask the police, but one of them confessed to having a thing for bling.

We could try appealing to his better nature, but they say there's not an authentic bone in his body, and that his heart was made in China.

Janet Lees

Collapsing is a lot like anything else when you think about it

Collapsing is like standing up in reverse. Reverse collapsing is not a negative – think feet on floor, bottom on chair, the back firm and straight. Collapsing is less of a crumple and more of a slither, like a drunk slumping slowly down a wall. A wall collapsing is more than a simple kitchen-sink drama – think subsidence, think demolition, whatever you do don't think bomb. Bomb is like the collapsing elephant in the room, the thing we think about but don't mention, like aging – you hope it will never happen. Unlike aging the probability is somewhat slimmer. Collapsing is a slimmer version of bomb, the thing that we secretly dread. Dread lurks on every street corner, but we try to keep it at bay. Some of us keep it at bay by watching the news. The news allows us to feel like we are in control. We are not in control. We are not in control of our own collapsing. Some might say that we are not in control of anything; that it all comes down to luck or God. God is a collapsing concept that so far hasn't got us anywhere except into trouble.

Julia Webb

Chest

Jake said he'd give tea-chest bass a go. That year he played drums in an experimental rock band was the happiest of his life – a pro drummer who'd drummed for Chuck Berry said he was the best 'non-drummer' he'd ever heard. None of the stress of remembering lyrics. But the heavy, single string blistered his index finger. He took to wearing a gardening glove and liked the sense of protection, of hugging, the kind that clung. A rubber glove gave an interesting, strangled tone for sliding notes. A surgical glove got an even better twang but broke easily. He kept a shoe box of options. Soon it was a sack. He needed to be able to get at them more easily at gigs. He built a rack that looked like so many wind chimes, but they were gloves. He started wearing makeup, KISS meets Cleopatra. Audiences cheered the fashionista director of entertainment, waited in fascination as he re-clad his hands. The fatal moment, he sliced a finger open with a band saw making another frame. No amount of bandaging or layering of gloves would assuage.

Owen Bullock

Mountain Hare

"I feel most coloured when I am thrown against a sharp white background." — Zora Neale Hurston

i've watched the snowline slide up the mountain's flanks for days, whiteness receding with the spring warmth. today, i see a mountain hare sitting in its form under frozen fists of bracken, eating the last of the snow, as if eating snow will keep it white. this is a poem about whiteness, its inevitability, but i'm using the misdirection of the hare because there's a metaphor there. i see the hare because its white pelage is no longer camouflage. its phenotypic crypsis has been compromised. which is another way of saying it is no longer thrown against a sharp white background and its body is now as visible as that Dürer sketch. the weight of humanity has shifted the tilt of the earth on its axis and i want this hare to teach me that whiteness is really only the accident of melaninic north and the dangers of vitamin deficiency – there is nothing supreme about a compass point.   so, mountain hare, tell me why you bury your tongue in the snow and eat: why do you desire whiteness? is it because you need to fit in, to survive, to hide? is this about survival? is it because, if you go brown, you won't get that job? is it to avoid getting shot in your long back? is your birth certificate in doubt? is it because when *La La Land* was mistakenly announced *Best Picture* at the Oscars in 2017, people didn't really doubt the result because the winner, *Moonlight*, is about the life of a gay black man? is this why you eat snow? is your ghost-whiteness merely a privileged species of willed forgetfulness?   chew it over. i'll wait.

Samuel Tongue

Snuskit

The shore is just not nice. Good. The hashed basalt is black and all the rubberduckery of the Atlantic is blown up here – a bloated seal and sometimes skull, fishboxes and buoys, a cummerbund of rotting kelp. The wind topples me, punches me gently into a pool. Beyond, strafed with hail, the sea teems like TV, with frayed aerial. I step back onto my tuffet, boots pooled in buttery light. The wind punches me gently into a pool. I'm doing my best impression of a gull – pesky, pitied, lonely, greedy, hopping up and down on my tuffet. The wind punches me gently into a pool.

Jen Hadfield

A Room with a View

Around the hospital's closed courtyard the *lungi*-clad man ran and ran, barefoot and with cleaver raised. Under a square sky the chased chicken ran helter-skelter and my eyes raced. Clutching veranda rails from the room in the typhoid ward, I dizzied seeing that desperate dance in the yard below – of headless bird, of headless hunter. The sedated sky held no escape as waves of horror swamped the room. Feeling the lime-washed walls, I stumbled back to the high bed in the middle of the room and clutched the starched stiff bed-clothes. The smell was antiseptic and strange, hospital-inhumane.

Debjani Chatterjee

Street Party 1935

Recreation Ground, Ufford Street / Mitre Road

A moon on her hat, a feather on his, mock nippies tied together
with one ribbon, a flower bigger than the wearer's head, a couple
of paper crowns, a pointy, jester, pirate hat, three round-head tin
hats – little soldiers, all cut up with bunting.

Big bowls of stuff to serve into smaller bowls, and plates of
triangular sandwiches, plates with sausage rolls, a slice of ham,
slab cake and cups of tea with milk and sugar and it's all for the
kiddies – only for the kiddies, and all sliced by bunting.

The ladies, in pinafores with waitress hats but no buttons,
overblown bosoms and cardigans ablaze. Her heavy coats. Her
outmoded hats. Her busy busy. Her standing with the girls,
watching the kiddies and all those slices of bunting.

More men than you notice at first – suited and watching – from
the back. Except him, with both hands on the teapot, must be
enamel, must be red, playing mum. Him with an accordion
and beret. Him with a megaphone in his hand. All cut up with
bunting.

And you, who said you could stand on the seat, eat that yet, cry,
stare up at the sun, wander off with your thumb in your mouth
– and you, who said you could look creased by sleep walking into
the wind, who said you could take your hat off, who said you
could get cut up by bunting?

Anna Robinson

Ridgeway

Near Uffington

It was a hard ascent up to the chalklands into places that didn't know water. Then stepping into a sky bigger than anything except mind, and how we live sometimes as if the sky were not big enough to swallow us whole, holy, but that day we parted the tranches of barley like waves in a field canted towards the horizon and knew that we could fly, upwards into the scudding blue intervals; and later though you were a foot away I could hear your heartbeat through the chalk and the day breathing the greengold barley and the silvermauve grasses and little downland flowers that knew something of blue and the skylark kiting its song, and below us the white horse dreaming in its long slow sleep as it has for millennia and the sky came down anyway – a moment when we might enter someone else's life, and remember.

Roselle Angwin

Chipping

In the end the fall was an abstract event, piece by tiny piece picked out with scissors and butter knives, enough to allow a view without Renate's kitchen chair. The People's Police were smiling, wanting to be part of this too – the clubs, the squatting scene – Friedrichstrasse Station no longer Palace of Tears. As free men they will take pride in the world, as Berliners overstep the mark. Hands pressed against the graffiti and the warning signs took years to take effect; winter on that side, summer on this, it was an artistic staging of occupation, perverse normality to formalise a generation's right to order and separation. When she moves her place of residence in '68, my mother erects a border of her own, is determined to treat it as such, with all its consequences, long after The Wall no longer exists.

Nic Stringer

The Flayed Fish

On a glass-fronted bookshelf in my great uncle's porch there lived a 35lb carp in a frame. I say lived but of course it was dead, angled from a lake and silenced like someone whose heart is in trouble and is put in a coma to give them a chance.

Because the glass was mildewed and opaque, the fish looked to be encased in ice. It had been caught in a body of water belonging to The Family Home. My uncle was always carping on about The Family Home, which is now an ailing leisure club. The lake served as a fridge in the days before fridges and the children would skate on it in the winter.

The first time he told me the tale, I saw that underwater world of the past through his clear lens, its iridescent shock plucked out, still twitching in an attempt to escape its skin. Each time he told it, something deteriorated, imperceptible at first – its fins split and tinged in sepia as though air was getting in and colour seeping out – and every time he lost the thread or I couldn't quite catch it, he'd say, *Not much point carping on.*

I can't recall the details now – the cast of the weather or what his father said – but I still know where it came from and at night feel its cold still weight in my chest.

Becky Cherriman

Halb null

It occurred to me to ask the time. She said *Halb null*. Half an hour to zero. How did it get so late? We had done nothing, only dallied in the café in the square, eating bread and artichokes, using up time to no purpose, and yet with a long journey to make. Halb null, and we had not even set out!

There were road blocks, long queues of traffic out of the city. At a standstill alongside a wide flat field, we watched circus performers rehearsing, tossing fire-sticks to each other in complicated patterns and interweavings. Sometimes they missed their catches, laughed as the fire-sticks fell harmlessly at their feet. It was late and they were only rehearsing, there was no sense of urgency or concern among them. But for us, time had slipped through our fingers, it seemed that we might never get back.

Helen Tookey

The Walk

He drifts away from the house, glances back every so often, admiring its honeyed stone. Framed through trees and under leaf-lace, it re-assuringly re-appears. A memory slides in, brings back hide & seek, him breaking free from his mother's arms or his father's hand, inciting panic when momentarily he'd disappear from view; their faces coming alive each time he stepped into plain sight.

He walks the lane, as far as the road and turns. His gaze is a butterfly's flit over wild flower meadow – the foxgloves, he knows, but too many cannot be named. He stops to address those he does: buttercups, daisies, dandelions and cow-parsley scattered in abundance, as if his mother's precious doilies had escaped her dresser; had fancied a picnic. A line of poplars, tall and thin, ten green bottles (empty or full?) draw his eyes down to the main road. He swings round to salute the majestic oak that stands alone, solemn, sentry-like. In full June bloom, firm-rooted and self-assured. When he leaves tomorrow, it might be for the last time, he will steal his brother's boots, but today he walks to imprint a picture in his mind, one he will hold forever, not just the way out, but the way back home.

Therese Kieran

The Stroll

A dreamy morning, sky empty and a wakening breeze. We ambled out, a brief jaunt, a pick-me-up before coffee, headed down to the river, kept walking, talked a little. A boat went past. 'Let's keep going,' I said, and you seemed uncertain, but we did. Pastures, meadows, roadside paths. We kept on, the land unfolding itself, and we ascended hills, perspiration leaking inside our shirts. When the clouds and rain arrived I sat inside a cave, came outside to find you'd gone, your body moving down the hill and beyond my anxious calls. I could see you weren't coming back, so I walked on, into rain and valleys, feet sore, mouth hot, famished, weary. Seasons rolled past each other, autumn was soft and brown, winter was narrow and stubborn. Summer came again, eventually, and all the time I trained my eyes on the horizon, sad that you weren't there to share the journey, and knowing something had shifted forever. Strangers were kind, they took me in and gave me bread. I washed when I could. My beard grew wild, with streaks of grey. Sometimes, at night, I glimpsed foxes, badgers, bats, rodents. They were quick. They willed themselves to go on. I caught boats, wandered into other nations. Words spelt towns that felt wrong, I made friends and lost them, earned money and spent it, became a tramp, a beggar, rootless and sad, all the time keeping my eyes on the horizon, kicking at the earth for years, wanting to escape it, but bound by it, and coming, each evening, to a town square with a half-hearted fountain, or a pub, or an alley, or woodland, a temporary home to stand in, and resolved to not want any more.

Miles Salter

Black House, Great Berneray, Western Isles

" 's na h-igheanan nam 'badan sàmhach/a' dol a Clachan mar o thus"
— July, 2016

Squat dwelling of the old ways, stone buttock bared to the grey Sound of Harris; roof timbers exposed; thatch a scalp with alopecia. From the roof-tree (sea-salvaged beams, white & crooked as the shins of old men), sway handmade ropes – doll's hair ragged by Atlantic winds.

Driech hole for shelter. Mud floor tramped by Sheep, who stamp in at a door jilted on hinges. Here, the walls' depth measures roughly a woman's length when knocked down, arms out, resisting eviction.

Modernity's groomed the place in other ways too. But the panel-clad interior has been reduced to a jumble of tongue & groove littering rooms – its greens, pinks & creams bruised by the elements. Tangle of rot & weather.

A stove made the warm bosom of this house; now it's a rusting hulk slumped by which the sole settee is a broken defiance of springs, stuffing of horse-hair plucked out for nests. One culprit Wren flees through a window's jagged teeth, where Nettles jostle like aggrieved kin barred from re-entering.

Proud, bristling emblem of Scotland, Thistles guard these ruins &, a stone's throw back across the cropped machair, other homes that formed the clachan. Two have been restored for tourists exploring the island, their walls fresh white. And like the lead-hemmed gowns of Victoria & entourage (who cruised within sight of the famine-blighted isles in 1847), their thatch is weighted against gales.

Secured with blue polyprop onto the coarse skirts of each, perhaps three dozen flat, pendulous stones. And do the visitors see them, these petrified livers & kidneys? Hung out to dry here, so many dull livers & lungs, and the countless grey, grey hearts of the emigrants – the vital Gaelic cut away.

Helen Moore

Porous

No such thing as bad weather for walking, just unsuitable clothes. He was kitted out in Gore-Tex and wore top brand gaiters and carried walking poles. She wore a merino layer under an elderly anorak. It poured with rain, but they didn't mind, because they knew they would dry off later. When they got back, they hung his jacket to drip into the bath, and she stripped off her wet jumper. She was soaked to the skin. Even her bra and pants were drenched. Then, no matter how hard she towelled herself she could not get dry. And when she peeled off her skin, the ligaments and tendons dissolved into mush, and the flesh was saturated and separated like strands of wet hair. Her soggy bones drifted apart. She floated like seaweed. It is my fault, she thought; my skin is too thin and I have become porous. He scooped her up and draped her over the radiator while he waited for the kettle to boil.

Hannah Stone

What did the orange gain

when it lost its 'n'? Orotundity and foreignness – an orange is rounder than a *naranja*. It announces its roundness at the very beginning, out loud in black type: O.

But the 'n' didn't just drop off and fall away, a curl of peel. It slid across into negative space, no-man's land, the indefinite article. There it is, in the middle: empty vessel without so much as an outline around it.

You can't throw a circle off-balance, but a painting needs a tipping movement. Something to set the eye rolling, ball on a see-saw. Teeter-totter, the clatter of utensils. Cutting-board, and the knife's an indicator. Spin it like a needle and see whose heart it points to.

Not many murder stories happen in kitchens, despite all the knives, the opportunities. Or maybe they're disembodied – the murders, I mean. Acid, or the ones that slowly boil away until the pan's burnt dry. Spices whose oils evanesce into the atmosphere…

the vanishing's the point.

Anna Reckin

Observation #6

The only light in the room comes from the screen of her laptop. Her eyes are fatigued. She has been here beyond the time she gave herself. Three ambulances have passed her building tonight. There was no noise from the people upstairs. She would like to have a cat, she thinks, but the regulations on the keeping of animals is clear. Somewhere on the pavement down below people are running. There are always people running. She stands at the window to see. Inside her ear is the sound of water. Inside her ear is the sound of someone in the water.

Mark Ryan Smith

Tinkers' Fires

When I was a child I loved to play in the ashes of tinkers' fires. Inscrutable abandoned trinkets, treasure of old nails beautiful in their purple rust, fragile, crumbling in my fingers, they were holy relics, riddles in horse-shoe heel-plate, D-rings, buckles, conjuring the sour dust of sweat, hoof-beat, harness races from the blue-black cinders. Sometimes a mud-caked pony chained to a stake grazed forlornly nearby. Be careful, Geordie Whittle said, pissing into the ashes so I would not burn myself. Muggers, Flee-b'-neets, Taggarine Men and their women. We scarcely saw them. Their glamorous residues glowed in the embers. From the bruise-red pit-brick end of the colliery row, the cold, charred circle of their fires became a mystery I longed to enter; out of which I summoned, like a cave-painter, in charcoal and ochre, the hot dung smell, the hoof-print, of whatever is ephemeral, fugitive, itinerant, just passing through.

Katrina Porteous

[Untitled]

Rain breaks, fork scrapes over and finally pierces yolk and the yellow sun spills out. You leave. Our torque overcomes inertia, and we end in ambiguity as ever. Anna had been killed. And in the days after her world ended we cried and held hands at the first memorial, legs not quite connecting with pavement, pulled along, numb, by the tides. In sleep you called out to me in your mother tongue, forgotten upon waking. You left me with only stories for strangers, an opening line, 'I once had a lover who'…

I once had a lover who fried eggs for breakfast and we ate them in the garden and the sun was unbearable.

Sophia Knight

"To Germany"

In evenings I thin towards the lighthouse. Gaze out at the grey-to-grey of sea-sky. Detail the glints of anchored ships and imagine the industry aboard. I put a stethoscope to other people's *gannin*, the rhythms of pitch and tone. I say hello out of time and receive closed lips, eyebrows like the cliffs above which a fret veils their sandy sun.

Incomer.

The sea spumes and fits. On other days I decode palimpsests of footprints on their brown beach and feel my keening. The embalming solitude. It's just a dog who'll decide I belong. Will streak for me one blustery evening and I'll crash these keen hands over his keen snout. That evening I head towards the lighthouse, spot the sign "To Germany" and don't I stretch and stretch and

Sarah Dobbs

Search Party

We said we'd never come back to Carrick but here we are pitching our tents, well away from the rushes and reeds. Eamon's pulled up in his rally car and here's Len with his smokes and beers, followed by Gavin with a box of torches. Cat's famous lurcher is burying a bone while Luke O'Mahony is flying his drone over a field of meadowsweet. And here comes Menno and here comes Graeme all dressed up in their running gear. St Jerome, with his pen and quill, who arrived last night, is supping his ale and cupping his ear hoping to translate the river's tale. Even God's shown up with his whoopee cushion and a tome of jokes. There's brother Robert with his sad eyes and, to pass the time, *Risk* and *Twister*. And next to the tree, Stacey's setting up a coconut shy. Grainne and Jenny are painting faces while Annett's limbering up for the wheelbarrow race. We said we'd never come back to Carrick but here we are – almost a crowd! Pitching our tents, stitching our hearts, well away from the rushes and reeds.

Maggie Sawkins

Woodcut

Walking home through the soft-rumbling city – Peckham shading to Camberwell – the tone shifts, furry growls rising and falling, showing their teeth. In a street-lit car park a large fox is finishing the remains of a discarded takeaway (chips and what looks like part of a burger). Silent. It's the cats that are growling: maybe ten, a feral gang all hackles and hisses, edging in then backing away, lawful. Fox is oblivious, alone with its kill in the middle of a night-filled acre, the village asleep, the bypass breathing slow.

Mark Granier

Eldest

Lean forward in shadow. The room is corridor opening into square, passage and purpose.

On the distant bed, a spill of mottled flesh, the white cotton gown fallen to little use. You gape in the doorway. His body is positioned away, toward the window. You stare until he calls, calls you into mutual shame.

Now you must gentle. The mind, relieved, packs away its unfinished question. The bowl of green gelatin has no scent. You hold it to your nose as he draws the cloth up with a tug, his grasp like a bird's.

No, not shame. Not now. Though he doesn't know it, he will be glad when you sit down at last. This is your father. The room is white and inescapable.

Carrie Etter

Reed Bunting

DESCRIPTION Wickerwork jolts, dark and buff, being over-wings and coverts, greater primary, greater secondary, median and undertail, a tight space of basic plumage, bastard wing, mantle, tertials, buff to rufous, buff to ravelled brown (and delicately wickered) remembering the importance of containment. *Male summer male winter adult female and juvenile* helmet of black, streaked also on breast, cheek stripe and white below, buff supercilia. Winter moulted, faded, head-pattern obscured by rufous-buff tips, collar and throat just visible. Compilation of midge and grass-seed worked into a thatch of buff and rufous, black and white, off-white and faded feathering. BEHAVIOUR Jerky flight and low, low perches on stem, flicks wings, opens tail, works the reed that works the water, tiny ripples, disappears into low and open sky. A dreary song of wheezy notes wheezily formed and very few notes and poorly performed. RANGE Adheres to the reed, plays for the wetland to follow, plays on its reed with its dreary notes, visits the house at night, the wetland follows. HABITAT Eutrophic seep between club rushes, frost bunching the thatch. The edge of carr. COMPARE this fist of reedstems, this seed-head blown from its stalk.

James Goodman

Occupation Road

We had enough for a couple of weeks, tins of beans, tins of fruit. We tried to pass the time although all the clocks had stopped. We shuffled cards, their flat patterns and quaint queens soothing. We built transistors from scratch but they picked up nothing but hiss. Everything tasted of tin; I worried it was coming from inside me. You were certain they'd erect cities on our garbage, write sagas in a language we'd never live to speak. The train stammered over the tracks at dusk, cargo scuttling to the far districts.

Tamar Yoseloff

High Noon

At this time shadows lose their social utility. They point neither to future nor past, neither back at the morning nor ahead, towards night. Selfishly, they gaze straight down into themselves, those fascinating depths.

Due to this shadowy irresponsibility, the world at this hour occasionally loses its sense of time. In the bright sunshine, around the axles of the shadows, it comes to an abrupt standstill. The flickering in the treetops stops; washing freezes on clotheslines; up on the road a car halts without using its brakes; and in a doorway, a calling woman stands paralysed, her open mouth filling with sky.

Meanwhile, high in the air a group of crows has been trapped. With looks of genuine shock on their faces, they hang in front of the sun like insects caught in amber. Far below, on the motionless field, their shadows lie like punctuation marks.

Fortunately for all concerned, the effect doesn't last. The shadows suddenly remember their obligation to civilisation and duly begin to lean in the general direction of afternoon. Trees bend, washing billows, the car lurches forward, the woman's voice breaks free of her mouth, and the crows flap away through the windy brightness.

The crow shadows, however, pause for a few instants: they tremble but hesitate, as if they've developed a taste for introspection. Then, possibly with some regret, they follow their dark birds over the horizon.

Robert Powell

Square of Light: The Artist is Present 1

A table in an atrium; a square of light. Two chairs at the table face each other – the artist in one, the other empty, an open invitation. Anyone, from anywhere, can sit with her, for as long or as little as they like. Over the course of three months, the artist looks into more than a thousand pairs of eyes. Halfway through the performance she takes the table away. Without a plane on which to lean, or slump or rest, the viewers become the viewees. Some of them cry. Not only are their faces exposed, but their legs or the absence of them. They become a body, not just a section of one and if they have ghosts for limbs, they become a story of that body. They don't tell her and she doesn't ask. There is no table anymore, no speaking, no leaning on elbows, no hidden shifting of shoes, just looking. Lives leak, itch, burn, smile, wince, blink, twitch, close, open, sleep, wake, stutter through their eyes. She catches and collects every drop; becomes a diary of what they don't say.

Jane Monson

The Danish Vote

came as weary leaders called to seal the borders of the Balkans, the foothills of the Carpathians and shores of the Dalmatians. Under new laws, they seized the corners of every foreign field, the brambly brims and crinkle-cut brinks where, year on year, young couples had been betrothed. Armies soon rounded up the lower bourns and closest contours. They took diameters, deep dividing lines, the easternmost edges where exhausted enemies had ceased the fire, happy to get their hands on natural depressions and elevations, glad to enclose enclaves and grant no stays. They cracked down hard on extremities where young children were buried, expropriated the flanks and frontiers, blocked the gateways to graveyards. Only gusts remained. Skirting highest hems, police arrested the hawthorn hedges, impounded islands and distant isthmuses, grabbed the jaggedy bits jutting out, cutting them off completely. They occupied outermost reaches, arrested picket fences, pillaging the porous periphery, reducing it to a powder. Over-running ravines and quartz quarries, they took A-roads and B-roads, left well alone the rusting lorries. Settlements were sequestered at the tailend of nowhere, not to mention the thalwegs, thresholds and tombolos; wherever the displaced survived. They uncovered the underbelly of umpteen verges and built a vast wall to silence the waterfall, locked each emergency exit to the margin of peace over yonder.

Paul Stephenson

In January 2016 Denmark encated a new law allowing police to seize refugee's assets.

Hold the Baby

They said she had to hold the baby so she held the baby even though she had no notion why she held it, him or her. They said she couldn't look to see so in her mind she thought of it as both, a Jenny and a James, and she knew it wasn't right but there was nothing more to say. They said they'd run some tests while she was holding it, experiments of a sort, but she was not so clear on what sort. Perhaps they measured angles, how she held it, how it sat there. Maybe they counted breaths, hers and its, or maybe blood flow or pressure, with machines she couldn't see. Maybe they wired up her brain and knew what she was thinking, feeling. Some time had passed, maybe minutes, and then she wanted to drop the baby. Not hard, not on the floor, just to not hold it any more.

Tania Hershman

All The Men I Never Married No. 34

I walked all over Leicester with you we walked from Braunstone to Braunstone town we walked to the clock tower and back again we walked along the canal and ran away from a man who pulled out his flaccid thing and waved it apologetically in our direction we walked the length of Braunstone Lane we walked the length of Narborough Road you showed me where you went fishing last summer before I knew you we walked to your house and you opened your fridge and showed me the maggots squirming in a tub and one had escaped but nobody cared not even your mum

you showed me your dad's fish tank in a month it was gone because he was bored of it you showed me the aviary he'd built himself the tiny and beautiful birds which lived there in two months he was bored of it and it was gone you showed me his pigeon loft you went to a scrap yard and begged for wood built yourself a pigeon loft you hated reading and writing but you built a loft and painted it and built the boxes and trained the birds to come to your hands to drop from the sky when you called once we went to town on our bikes and cycled home again you had pigeons stuffed down your coat with rings around one leg who'd forgotten the way back home and were living feral

we walked to Aylestone Meadows and scared ourselves near the cooling tower we walked through Mossdale Meadows you swung across the brook on a rope swing we crossed a motorway to get to the woods you didn't care about fences or gates or public rights of way or motorway regulations we thought nobody had ever walked there because there was no path and everything was the deepest green and the smell was earth and rotting wood the only sound the distant singing of the motorway we walked to rehearsal and you waited while I played *Last of the Summer Wine I Dreamed a Dream* then we walked back again we walked to the cinema at

Meridian the walk was the best bit we walked to Franklin Park and sat on the swings and ate bags of sweets covered in sugar you killed wasp after wasp as they hovered and sketched their way around the paper bag you were the only one of us who dared to walk across the climbing frame without using your hands we walked to a forgotten pond in the grounds of a school collected baby frogs and set them to slow motion races along a log stared for hours into the murky depths of the water watched the water boatman skim across the surface and returned each day to watch the late tadpoles grow legs sometimes I wasn't allowed to see you every day

the last summer we walked to a field where the grass was chest height lay down watched the sun make its way across the sky did those things to one another I'm imagining it I must be imagining it that there was ever a man on horseback who stood on top of a hill who watched as we rolled around in that sweet smelling grass which trapped the heat which hid us from the world which hid us from everything but the sky maybe my heart made him up maybe my mind made him up we were young we stayed still as if staying still meant he wouldn't see we covered our faces you held my head to your shoulder when we looked again there was no horseman there was only you and I do you remember the horseman

Kim Moore

Notes

'Black House, Great Berneray, Western Isles' by Helen Moore – A blackhouse is a traditional type of thatched house once common in the Scottish Highlands & Hebrides.

" 's na h-igheanan nam 'badan sàmhach/a' dol a Clachan mar o thus" are lines from Sorley MacLean's poem 'Hallaig'. He translates them from the Gaelic as: "and the girls in silent bands/ go to Clachan as in the beginning."

A clachan is a traditional village settlement.

The quote by Jeanette Winterson that prefaces Winston Plowes's 'The Rooms Behind the Eyes' is taken from https://www. goodreads.com/quotes/85752-do-you-wake-up-as-i-do-having-forgotten-what

Zora Neale Hurston's quote that precedes Samuel Tongue's 'Mountain Hare' is taken from *How it Feels to be Colored Me* (New York: The World Tomorrow, 1928).

'A Room with a View' by Debjani Chatterjee – A *lungi* is a cloth wrapped around the waist.

'Snuskit' by Jen Hadfield – *Snuskit*: in a sulky frame of mind.

Acknowledgements

Luke Kennard's 'A.1.' was first published in *Truffle Hound* (Verve, 2018).

Natalie Whittaker's 'Boat Party' was first published in the pamphlet *Shadow Dogs* (Ignition Press, 2018).

Linda Black's 'My mother is locked in a jar of ginger' was first published in *Inventory* (Shearsman, 2008).

Paul Munden's 'From *The Encyclopaedia of Forgotten Things*' was first published as 'Before the music' in *Rabbit* 19 (2016), then as part of 'From *The Encyclopaedia of Forgotten Things*' *Chromatic* (UWA Publishing, 2017).

Mary Jean Chan's 'Dress' was first published in *The Scores* 2 (Spring 2017).

John Freeman's 'Apples on a Tree' was first published in *White Wings* (Contraband, 2013).

Patrica Debney's 'High Tide at the Spit' was first published in *Littoral* (Shearsman, 2013).

Geraldine Clarkson's 'My Mother, the Monsoon' was first published in *Primers Volume 1* (Nine Arches Press, 2016) and in *Declare* (Shearsman, 2016).

Helen Ivory's 'The Tales' was first published in *Maps of the Abandoned City* (SurVision books).

Ceinwen E. Cariad Haydon's 'Purple' was first published in the on-line magazine, *Algebra of Owls*: https://algebraofowls.com/

Heidi Williamson's 'Hellbox' was first published in *The Print Museum* (Bloodaxe, 2016) and is reproduced here with kind permission from the author and publisher.

Inua Ellams's 'Ghetto van Gogh' was first published in *Ten, The New Wave,* ed. Karen McCarthy Woolf (Bloodaxe, 2014) and is reproduced with kind permission of the author.

Jenna Clake's 'Bread, orange, aura' was first published in *The Tangerine* 5 (2018).

Lisa Matthews's 'Signal on' was first published as the prologue in *Callisto* (Red Squirrel Press, 2018).

Charlotte Eichler's 'The Coffin Calendars' was first published in *Blackbox Manifold* 19 (Winter 2017).

Ian Seed's 'The House that Jack Built' was first published in *Identity Papers* (Shearsman, 2016).

Anne Ryland's 'Running, I become' was commended in the Magma Poetry Competition 2018.

Simon Armitage's 'A New Career in a New Town' was first published in *Flit* (YSP, 2018) to celebrate the 40th Anniversary of the Yorkshire Sculpture Park (2017).

Mark Russell's 'I∧∧∧*' was first published in *the book of seals* (Red Ceilings Press, 2015).

Ágnes Lehóczky's 'Letter from Terry' was first published in *Swimming Pool* (Shearman, 2017).

Michael Loveday's 'Cups' was first published in *Under the Radar* 19 (July 2017).

Susie Campbell's 'Reef' was first published *Tears in the Fence* 67 (Winter/Spring 2018).

Janet Lee's 'The Geegaw Man' was first published in an anthology of winning poems from Tongues and Grooves Prose Poetry competition: *Bird Count, November* (Tongues and Grooves, 2018).

Julia Webb's 'Collapsing is a lot like anything else when you think about it' is forthcoming in *Threat* (Nine Arches Press, 2019).

Owen Bullock's 'Chest' is from the collection *Work & Play* (Recent Work Press, 2017) and was first published in *Stride* (April, 2017).

Jen Hadfield's 'Snuskit' was first published in *Nigh-No-Place* (Bloodaxe, 2008) and is reproduced here with kind permission of the publisher and author.

Debjani Chatterjee's 'A Room with a View' was first published in *Words Spit and Splinter* (Redbeck Press, 2009).

Anna Robinson's 'Street Party 1935' is forthcoming in *Whatsname St* (Smokestack, 2021).

Roselle Angwin's 'Ridgeway' was first published in *Bardo* (Shearsman, 2011).

Helen Tookey's 'Halb null' was first published in *Shearsman* 113-114 (Winter 2017-18).

Helen Moore's 'Black House, Great Berneray, Western Isles' was first published in *North Words Now* (2017), and is included in her latest collection, *The Mother Country* (Awen Publications, 2019).

Anna Reckin's 'What did the orange gain' was written in response to Geoffrey Robinson's *Dreaming Paintbrush Painting Number 11*, and first published in *Line to Curve* (Shearsman, 2018).

Mark Ryan Smith's 'Observation #6' is taken from a sequence of (mostly) prose poems called *Conflux*.

Maggie Sawkins's 'Search Party' was first published in *Many Skies Have Fallen* (Wild Mouse Press, 2018).

Mark Granier's 'Woodcut' was first published in the *And Other Poems* web journal 2013: https://andotherpoems. com/2013/12/10/mark-granier/

Carrie Etter's 'Eldest' first appeared in *The Weather in Normal* (UK: Seren; US: Station Hill, 2018).

Tamar Yoseloff's 'Occupation Road' was first published in *Shearsman* 117 & 118 (Winter 2018).

Jane Monson's 'Square of Light; The Artist is Present 1' was first published in *The Shared Surface* (Cinnamon, 2013).

Paul Stephenson's 'The Danish Vote' was first published in *The Fenland Reed* 5 (Autumn 2017).

Tania Hershman's 'Hold the Baby' was first published in *Butcher's Dog* magazine and is included in *Some Of Us Glow More Than Others* (Unthank Books, 2017).

Kim Moore's 'All the Men I Never Married No. 34' was first published in *The Rialto*.

About the Contributors

Astrid Alben is a poet and translator currently living in London. Her first collection, *Ai Ai Pianissimo* was published by Arc Publications in 2011. Her second collection, *Plainspeak*, will be published in 2019 by Prototype. Alben is a Rijksakademie Fellow and she was awarded a Wellcome Trust Fellowship 2014.

Nick Allen has recently twice been runner-up in poetry competitions based in Ireland: the Bangor Literary Journal, poems of 40 words or less; and the 2018 Hungry Hill Writers International competition, 'Poets meet Politics'. His first pamphlet, *the necessary line,* was published by Half Moon Books in October 2017.

Roselle Angwin is a Westcountry author and poet. She has written 13 books plus many articles, poems etc. She is the director of the Fire in the Head creative writing programme and also of The Wild Ways – a programme for the ecological imagination. Roselle is passionate about the connections between inner and outer landscapes, and the human and other-than-human.

Simon Armitage is a poet, playwright and novelist based in West Yorkshire. He is Professor of Poetry at the University of Leeds. In 2015, Armitage was elected to become Oxford Professor of Poetry, succeeding Geoffrey Hill. Armitage has received numerous awards for his poetry including the 2017 PEN America Award for Poetry in Translation. In 2018 he received the Queen's Gold Medal for Poetry. In 2019 he became Poet Laureate of the United Kingdom.

Liz Bahs was Writer-in-Residence at The Hambidge Center for Creative Arts and Sciences, Rabun Gap, GA, USA in 2018. She is a Teaching Fellow of English Literature and Creative Writing at University of Surrey and an Associate Lecturer of Creative Writing for The Open University. Her poetry can be found in *Greyhound*

Night Service (Maquette Press, UK 2018); her collection, *Stay Bones* is forthcoming with Pindrop Press (2019).

Becky Balfourth is an author living and writing poems, stories and poems in the Greater London area. Apart from writing she likes running and reading. She writes online at thesleevelessproject. wordpress.com and balfourthrbpoetry.wordpress.com.

Linda Black is a poet and visual artist. *The beating of wings* (Hearing Eye, 2006) was the PBS Pamphlet Choice for Spring 2007, when she also received an Arts Council Writer's Award. Her fourth collection *Slant* was published by Shearsman in 2016). Prose poem collections are *Inventory* and *Root* (Shearsman 2008 & 2011). *The Son of a Shoemaker* (Hearing Eye, 2012) consisting of collaged prose poems plus the author's illustrations. She teaches for the Poetry School and is co-editor of Long Poem Magazine, www.longpoemmagazine.org.uk

K. Blair is a bisexual poet, currently based in London. Primarily a page poet, she takes inspiration from her sexuality, folklore and her complicated relationship with religion. She is a proud member of London Queer Writers.

Owen Bullock was born and bred in Cornwall and moved to New Zealand in 1989. Bullock has won awards for his poetry and is widely published in New Zealand and overseas. He has been an editor of several magazines, including *Poetry NZ* and *Kokako*. He has published poetry, haiku, fiction and non-fiction. He currently teaches at the University of Canberra. Most recent publications are *Work & Play* (Recent Work Press, 2017) and *Semi* (Puncher & Wattmann, 2017). He has a website for his research into poetry and process, at poetry-in-process.com.

Sue Burge is a freelance creative writing and film studies lecturer based in North Norfolk where she creates pop-up poetry workshops for a wide range of students. Her debut pamphlet was *Lumière*

(Hedgehog Poetry Press). Sue's first full collection, *In the Kingdom of Shadows,* (Live Canon Poetry Press) explores the liminal spaces we inhabit both consciously and unconsciously. Both collections feature a number of prose poems. Sue runs a successful on-line writing course *The Writing Cloud.* More details at sueburge.uk

Jane Burn is a North East based artist and writer. Her poems have been featured in magazines such as *The Rialto, Under The Radar, Butcher's Dog, Iota Poetry* and *Crannog* as well as anthologies from the Emma Press, Beautiful Dragons, Emergency Poet and Seren. Her pamphlets include *Fat Around the Middle,* (Talking Pen) and *Tongues of Fire* (BLER Press). Her first collection, *nothing more to it than bubbles,* was published by Indigo Dreams.

Maggie Butt is a poet and novelist, with a background as a journalist and BBC TV documentary producer. Her fifth poetry collection was *Degrees of Twilight* (The London Magazine, 2015). She is an Associate Professor of Creative Writing at Middlesex University and a Royal Literary Fund Advisory Fellow. Her novel *The Prisoner's Wife* has just been accepted by Penguin for summer 2020 publication. See also maggiebutt.co.uk.

Anne Caldwell is based in West Yorkshire. She lectures in creative writing for the Open University and is undertaking a PhD in prose poetry at The University of Bolton. Anne's current poetry collection is *Painting the Spiral Staircase* (Cinnamon 2016). Her work has been anthologised in the UK and Australia. Her prose poetry was shortlisted in *The Rialto* pamphlet competition (2017) and won second prize in *Tongue and Grooves* prose poetry competition, 2018. Anne was awarded funding from The Arts Council of England to set up prose-poetry.uk

Susie Campbell is the author of *The Bitters* (Dancing Girl Press, 2014) and *The Frock Enquiry* (Annexe, 2015). Her work has appeared in the UK and internationally, e.g. *3AM, Tears in the Fence, Shearsman, Lighthouse* and *Cordite.* Two sequences of her prose poetry appeared in *Long Poem Magazine* (2017, 2018). She was a poet-in-residence for the 2017-18 Mellon-Sawyer Post-War Commemoration series and is studying for a PhD in prose poetry and working on her first full-length collection. Twitter at @susiecampbell and blog: susiecampbellwrites.wordpress.com

Mary Jean Chan is a poet, editor and academic from Hong Kong. She came Second in the National Poetry Competition and was shortlisted for the 2017 Forward Prize for Best Single Poem. Her debut pamphlet, *A Hurry of English*, was selected as the 2018 Poetry Book Society Summer Pamphlet Choice. Her poems have appeared in *The Poetry Review, Poetry London, PN Review, Ambit* and *The White Review.* Her debut collection will be published by Faber & Faber in July 2019. Mary Jean is a Lecturer in Creative Writing (Poetry) at Oxford Brookes University, and currently lives in London.

Debjani Chatterjee, MBE, FRSL is an Indian-born poet and writer based in Sheffield. Editor, translator, children's writer, RLF Fellow & creative arts therapist, she has written & edited over 65 books, including the poetry collections *Namaskar: New & Selected Poems, Words Spit & Splinter* and *I Was That Woman.* She has also edited award winning anthologies including *The Redbeck Anthology of British South Asian Poetry.*

Becky Cherriman is a writer, workshop leader and performer from Leeds. Published by Seren, *Mslexia, New Walk* and Bloodaxe, her poetry was commended in the Forward Prizes 2017. She has a pamphlet *Echolocation* and collection *Empires of Clay* and also writes fiction and for theatre. www.beckycherriman.

Jenna Clake's debut collection, *Fortune Cookie*, was awarded the Melita Hume Prize and shortlisted for a Somerset Maugham Award. In 2018, she received an Eric Gregory Award from the Society of Authors. A pamphlet of her prose poems, *CLAKE / Interview for,* was published by Verve Poetry Press in 2018.

Geraldine Clarkson's prose poems have been published in *This Line Is Not For Turning: An Anthology of Contemporary British Prose Poetry* (ed. Jane Monson, Cinnamon Press, 2011), and also feature in her three poetry pamphlets: *Declare* (Shearsman Books, 2016), a PBS Pamphlet Choice; *Dora Incites the Sea-Scribbler to Lament* (smith|doorstop, 2016), a Laureate's Choice; and *No. 25* (Shearsman Books, 2018).

Writer and visual artist, Claire Collison is an honouree of the inaugural Women Poets' Prize. She teaches and writes in a wide range of settings. Her first novel was a finalist in the Dundee Book Prize, and her short stories have been included in Bridport. Her poetry is widely published and was shortlisted for the 2016/17 Poetry Business Competition. Claire is currently Artist in Residence at the Women's Art Library.

Patricia Debney is a Reader in Creative Writing at the University of Kent. She has published four books of poetry, a novel and numerous poems and short stories in anthologies and journals as well as online. Her latest collection is *Baby* (Liquorice Fish Books, 2016) and her next book will be a memoir titled *#AboutTime*.

Kym Deyn is a poet, playwright and fortune teller based in the North East. They are in their third year at Durham University studying Classical Civilisations. They have been shortlisted for a number of awards including the Terry Kelly Poetry Prize and the West Yorkshire Playhouse 'Airplays' Competition. Most recently they were longlisted for the 2019 Outspoken Prize.

Sarah Dobbs is a lecturer in English and Creative Writing. Her novel *Killing Daniel* is out now from @UnthankBooks. She has been nominated for the Guardian's Not the Booker award and has taught on the Guardian Masterclass series, as well as at Manchester, Lancaster, Edge Hill and Sunderland University, where she is currently a full-time lecturer in Creative Writing. Her new novel, *The Sea Inside Me,* is due out in 2019 from Unthank.

Kristian Doyle is a writer who lives in Liverpool. He is currently at work on a novel.

Charlotte Eichler was born in Hertfordshire in 1982 and now lives in Yorkshire. She has an MA in Norse and Viking Studies and works as a bibliographer at the University of Leeds. Her poetry has been published in numerous magazines and anthologies, including *PN Review*, *The Rialto* and *Stand*. Her debut pamphlet, *Their Lunar Language*, was published by Valley Press in July 2018.

Inua Ellams was born in Nigeria and is an award-winning poet, playwright & founder of the Midnight Run. Identity, Displacement & Destiny are reoccurring themes in his work in which he mixes the old with the new, traditional with the contemporary. His books are published by Flipped Eye, Akashic, Nine Arches & Oberon.

Carrie Etter is an American expatriate who has been writing and publishing prose poems for over thirty years. She has published four collections of poetry, most recently *The Weather in Normal* (UK: Seren; US: Station Hill, 2018), and edited *Infinite Difference: Other Poetries by UK Women Poets* (Shearsman, 2010). She is Reader in Creative Writing at Bath Spa University.

Ailish Fowler graduated from Newcastle University in July 2017 with a BA degree in English Literature and Creative Writing, specialising in poetry. She now lives and works in London and continues to share her work on her blog, ailishfowler.co.uk

John Freeman's poem 'Exhibition' won the Bridport Prize in 2018. His books include *Strata Smith and the Anthropocene* (Knives Forks and Spoons), and *What Possessed Me* (Worple), which was the Wales Poetry Book of the Year, 2017. Earlier collections include *A Suite for Summer* (Worple), and *White Wings: New and Selected Prose Poems* (Contraband).

James Goodman grew up in Cornwall and now lives in Hertfordshire. His first collection of poems, *Claytown*, was published in 2011 by Salt. He is working towards a second collection provisionally titled *Stone Mountain Fairy Shrimp*.

Mark Granier's poems have appeared in numerous outlets in the UK and Ireland over the years, including the *Times Literary Supplement*, *The Irish Times*, *The Spectator*, *Poetry Review* and *The New Statesman*. Mark Granier's fourth collection, *Haunt,* was published by Salmon Poetry in 2015, and his *Ghostlight: New & Selected Poems* came out from the same publisher in 2017.

Jen Hadfield is a poet and artist. At the moment she is working on a fourth collection of poetry, provisionally titled *The Stone Age*, exploring neurodiversity, and a collection of essays. She is building a house in Shetland, very slowly. She currently tutors on Glasgow University's Creative Writing programme and was writer in residence in Charles Causley's house in Autumn 2018. Twitter: @hadfield_jen

Oz Hardwick is a writer, photographer, music journalist and occasional musician based in York. He has published seven poetry collections, most recently *The House of Ghosts and Mirrors* (Scarborough: Valley Press, 2017) and a prose poetry chapbook, *Learning to Have Lost* (Canberra: IPSI, 2018). Oz is Professor of English at Leeds Trinity University, where he leads the Creative Writing programmes.

Robert Harper's poetry has appeared in many journals and anthologies, including *The Interpreter's House, Acumen, Lonely Crowd, Ink Sweat and Tears, And Other Poems, New Welsh Review,* and *Marble Poetry.* He was Highly Commended in the Poetry Book Society Student Poetry Competition 2014. Robert is the editor of Bare Fiction Magazine and is currently undertaking a PhD at the University of Birmingham in space & parenthesis in the poetry of the Objectivists.

Ceinwen E. Cariad Haydon lives in Newcastle upon Tyne, UK, and writes short stories and poetry. She has been widely published in web magazines and in print anthologies. She graduated with an MA in Creative Writing from Newcastle University in 2017. She believes everyone's voice counts.

Tania Hershman's third short story collection, *Some Of Us Glow More Than Others,* was published by Unthank Books in May 2017, and her debut poetry collection, *Terms & Conditions,* by Nine Arches Press in July. Tania is also the author of a poetry chapbook and two short story collections, *My Mother Was An Upright Piano,* and *The White Road and Other Stories,* and co-author of Writing Short Stories: A Writers' & Artists' Companion (Bloomsbury, 2014). Tania is curator of short story hub *ShortStops* (www.shortstops.info), celebrating short story activity across the UK & Ireland, and has a PhD in creative writing inspired by particle physics. Website: taniahershman.com

Gaia Holmes lives in Halifax. She is a freelance writer and creative writing tutor who works with schools, libraries and other community groups throughout the West Yorkshire region. She has had two poetry collections published by Comma Press: *Dr James Graham's Celestial Bed* (2006) and *Lifting The Piano With One Hand* (2013). *Tales from the Tachograph* was a collaborative work with Winston Plowes (Calder Valley Poetry, 2017). Her third collection, *Where the Road Runs Out,* was published by Comma Press in Autumn 2018.

Helen Ivory is a poet and visual artist. Her fifth Bloodaxe Books collection, *The Anatomical Venus,* was published in May 2019. She edits the webzine *Ink Sweat and Tears* and teaches online for the NCW/UEA. Her chapbook, *Maps of the Abandoned City* (SurVision, 2019) houses 'The Tales'.

Haley Jenkins graduated with a Masters in Creative Writing from The University of Surrey. Her debut collection *Nekorb* was published by Veer Books in August 2017. As well as online publications, her work has appeared in three anthologies by Fincham Press and *Persona Non-Grata* by Fly on the Wall Press.

Luke Kennard is a poet and novelist. His books have been shortlisted for the Forward Prize, the Desmond Elliott Prize and the International Dylan Thomas Prize. He lectures in the School of English at the University of Birmingham. His fifth collection, *Cain* was published in June 2016 by Penned in the Margins and his pamphlet, *Truffle Hound* was published by Verve Poetry Press in September 2018.

Therese Kieran lives in Belfast. Her work has featured in various magazines and anthologies, been placed in competitions and twice long-listed for the Heaney Award. In 2016 she co-conceived and curated, Death Box, an exhibition of poetry and prose. Once a textile designer, she's now painting with words.

Sophia Knight is an undergraduate studying Philosophy at the University of Sheffield, currently residing in Oregon, USA. The ambiguity of prose poetry appeals to her as a space to explore questions of love, loss and kinship outside of heterosexual frameworks. Her poetry has appeared in Prism literary magazine and Hive South Yorkshire's *Wild Poetry* and *Halfway Smile* anthologies.

Janet Lees is based in the Isle of Man. She represented the island in the BBC Radio Poetry Postcards project which featured a poet from each of the Commonwealth nations. Her work has been published in a wide range of poetry magazines and anthologies and her poetry films selected for a several international festivals and prizes, including the Aesthetica Art Prize and Filmpoem. Her prose poetry was prize-winning in the Tongues and Grooves Prose Poem Competition 2018.

Ágnes Lehóczky's collections published in the UK are *Swimming Pool* (2017), *Pool Epitaphs and Other Love Letters* (2017), *Carillonneur*

(2014), *Rememberer* (2012) and *Budapest to Babel* (2008). She is the author of *Poetry, the Geometry of Living Substance* (2011) and the editor of *Wretched Strangers* (2018), *The World Speaking Back ... to Denise Riley* (2018) and the *Sheffield Anthology* (2012).

Michael Loveday's novella-in-flash *Three Men on the Edge,* a sequence of short-short stories drawing on techniques of prose poetry, was published by V. Press in 2018. '*He Said* / She Said', his debut poetry pamphlet, was published by Happen*Stance* Press in 2011. He lives in Bath.

Lisa Matthews is a poet, creative writing scholar and collaborative artist; her fourth collection, *Callisto* (Red Squirrel Press, 2018) is her first to be made entirely of prose poem sequences. Lisa lives by the sea in the northeast of England and takes underwater photographs. For more info visit: poetryfold.co.uk

Jane Monson is a Mentor for students with disabilities at the University of Cambridge and a creative writing tutor. She has hosted events and workshops at the Cambridge Film Festival, Festival of Ideas and Science Festival and enjoys working collaboratively across disciplines. She edited *This Line is Not for Turning* (Cinnamon, 2011) and *British Prose Poetry: The Poems Without Lines* (Palgrave, 2018). Solo prose poetry collections include *Speaking Without Tongues* (2010) and *The Shared Surface* (2013) and a third one is in the making.

Kim Moore's first collection *The Art of Falling* (Seren, 2015) won the 2016 Geoffrey Faber Memorial Prize. She won a Northern Writers Award (2014), an Eric Gregory Award (2011) and the Geoffrey Dearmer Prize (2010). She is currently a PhD candidate at Manchester Metropolitan University researching poetry and experiences of sexism.

Helen Moore is an award-winning ecopoet and socially engaged artist. She has published three poetry collections, including *Hedge*

Fund, And Other Living Margins (Shearsman, 2012) and *ECOZOA* (Permanent Publications, 2015), acclaimed as 'a milestone in the journey of ecopoetics'. Her recently published third collection, *The Mother Country* (Awen Publications, 2019), explores British colonial history and themes of personal, social and ecological dispossession. helenmoorepoet.com

Helen Mort is the author of two poetry collections with Chatto & Windus, *Division Street* (2013) and *No Map Could Show Them* (2016). Her first novel is *Black Car Burning* (Chatto, 2019). Helen is a Fellow of the Royal Society of Literature and teaches Creative Writing at the Manchester Writing School, Manchester Metropolitan.

Paul Munden has published five poetry collections, most recently *Chromatic* (UWAP, 2017), and four prose poetry chapbooks. He was director of the National Association of Writers in Education, 1994-2018, and is currently Adjunct Associate Professor at the University of Canberra, Australia, where he established the 'Poetry on the Move' festival.

Winston Plowes shares his floating home in Calderdale UK with his 17-year-old cat, Sausage. He teaches creative writing in schools, universities and to local groups while she dreams of Mouseland. His latest collection *Tales from the Tachograph* was published jointly with Gaia Holmes in 2018 by Calder Valley Poetry. www.winstonplowes.co.uk

Katrina Porteous was born in Aberdeen, grew up in Co. Durham and has lived for 30 years on the Northumberland coast. She is particularly interested in spoken poetry and has written extensively for radio. Her collections from Bloodaxe include *The Lost Music* (1996), *Two Countries* (2014) and *Edge* (forthcoming, 2019).

Robert Powell lives in York. He has published three collections of poetry – *Harvest of Light, All*, and *Riverain* (Valley Press, 2018), as well as *A Small Box of River* with artist Jake Attree, and two short films – *The River Speaks*, with Ben Pugh and *Source*, with Jan-Erik Andersson. His poem 'The Telling' won a commendation in the National Poetry Competition 2017.

Angela Readman's poems have won The Mslexia Competition, The Charles Causey and The Essex Prize. Her collection *The Book of Tides* is published by Nine Arches. Her stories have won The Costa Short Story Award & The National Flash Fiction Competition. Her collection *Don't Try This at Home* won The Rubery Book Award.

Anna Reckin is a poet and writer based in Norwich. Her second collection, *Line to Curve*, appeared from Shearsman in 2018, and she has had poems, essays and reviews published in *Poetry Wales, Jacket2, Long Poem Magazine*, and a selection in the anthology *Infinite Difference: Other Poetries by UK Women Poets*.

Anna Robinson is a poet from London. Her collections *The Finders of London*, which was nominated for the Seamus Heaney Poetry Centre Prize in 2011, and *Into the Woods* were published by Enitharmon. Her next collection *Whatsname Street* will be published by Smokestack in 2021.

Mark Russell is a teacher of Drama. He has an MLitt in Creative Writing from the University of Glasgow, and an MA in Theatre Studies from the University of Leeds. His publications include *Spearmint & Rescue* (Pindrop), *Shopping for Punks* (Hesterglock), ℵ *(the book of moose)* (Kattywompus), ℩ *(the book of seals)*, and *Saturday Morning Pictures* (both with Red Ceilings). His poems have appeared in *Stand, Shearsman, Blackbox Manifold, Butcher's Dog, The Scores, Poetry Salzburg Review,* and elsewhere. He lives in rural Scotland.

Anne Ryland has published two poetry collections: *Autumnologist* (shortlisted for The Forward Prize for Best First Collection) and *The*

Unmothering Class. Her poems have appeared in anthologies such as *Land of Three Rivers* (Bloodaxe), and in magazines including *Poetry Review, Oxford Poetry, The North, Agenda* and *Long Poem Magazine.*

Miles Salter is a musician and writer based in York. His work encompasses writing, event management, music gigs and work in educational settings. He likes Marmite, early Bruce Springsteen albums and Philip Larkin. He voted remain but will get over it.

Maggie Sawkins lives in Portsmouth, Hampshire where she has organised the Tongues & Grooves Poetry and Music Club since 2003. Her poetry collections include *Charcot's Pet* (Flarestack), *The Zig Zag Woman* (Two Ravens Press), *Zones of Avoidance* (Cinnamon Press), and Many Skies Have Fallen, (Wild Mouse Press). In 2014 she won the Ted Hughes Award for New Work in Poetry for her live literature production, *Zones of Avoidance.* zonesofavoidance.wordpress.com

Ian Seed's collections of prose poems include *New York Hotel* (2018), *Identity Papers* (2016), and *Makers of Empty Dreams* (2014) (Shearsman). *New York Hotel* was a *TLS* 2018 *Book of the Year.* He is a contributor to *British Prose Poetry: The Poems Without Lines,* ed. Jane Monson (Palgrave Macmillan, 2018).

Mark Ryan Smith's work has appeared in various places, including *New Writing Scotland, Snakeskin, Northwords Now, PN Review* and *Ink Sweat & Tears.* He lives in the Shetland Isles.

Paul Stephenson grew up in Cambridge. He took part in the Jerwood/Arvon mentoring scheme and has three pamphlets: *Those People* (Smith/Doorstop, 2015), *The Days That Followed Paris* (HappenStance, 2016) and *Selfie with Waterlilies* (Paper Swans Press, 2017). He is co-curating Poetry in Aldeburgh 2019 and blogs at paulstep.com.

Hannah Stone has an MA in Creative Writing from Leeds Trinity University and two collections *Lodestone,* (Stairwell Books, 2016) and *Missing Miles* (Indigo Dreams Publishing, 2017). Forthcoming in 2019 are an inaugural pamphlet for Maytree Press (*Swn y Morloi on Pen-Caer*) and a collaboration with Rosemary Mitchell, *Holding up Half the Sky*. Her Penthos Requiem received its premiere performance in Leeds in October 2018 (penthos.uk). She convenes the poets/composers forum for Leeds Lieder festival and the Wordspace spoken word event in Horsforth.

Nic Stringer was highly commended in the Forward Prizes 2018 for *A day that you happen to know* (Guillemot Press). Poetry, art and film have appeared in anthologies and journals including *The Forward Book of Poetry, Magma, Structo, The Interpreter's House* and *@Arsonista*. Nic also organises readings and collaborations (corruptedpoetry.com).

George Szirtes was born in Hungary in 1948. His first book of poems, *The Slant Door* (1979) won the Faber Prize. He has published many since then, *Reel* (2004) winning the *T S Eliot Prize*, for which he has been twice shortlisted since. His latest book of poetry is *Mapping the Delta* (Bloodaxe 2016) and his memoir of his mother, *The Photographer at Sixteen*, is published by MacLehose this year.

Samuel Tongue has published two poetry pamphlets; *Stitch* (Tapsalteerie, 2018), *Hauling Out* (Eyewear, 2016) and appears in numerous magazines and anthologies. He held a Scottish Book Trust *New Writers Award* in 2013. Samuel is currently co-editor of *New Writing Scotland* and poetry editor at the *Glasgow Review of Books;* he is also Project Coordinator at the Scottish Poetry Library and lectures in Religion, Literature, and Culture at the University of Glasgow.

Helen Tookey was born near Leicester in 1969. She currently teaches Creative Writing at Liverpool John Moores University.

Her debut full-length collection, *Missel-Child* (Carcanet, 2014) was shortlisted for the 2015 Seamus Heaney Centre for Poetry Prize. Her pamphlet *In the Glasshouse* was published by HappenStance in 2016. Her second Carcanet collection, *City of Departures*, is forthcoming in July 2019 and has been shortlisted for the 2019 Forward Prize.

Julia Webb lives in Norwich, UK where she teaches creative writing, works for Gatehouse Press and is a poetry editor for Lighthouse. Her poem "Sisters" was highly commended in the 2016 Forward Prize. In 2018 she won the Battered Moons Poetry Competition. Her first collection *Bird Sisters* was published by Nine Arches Press in 2016. Her second collection *Threat* is published by Nine Arches Press in 2019.

Natalie Whittaker's debut pamphlet *Shadow Dogs* is published by ignitionpress. Her poems have also been published in *Poetry News*, *Brittle Star*, *Aesthetica Creative Writing Annual*, and *#MeToo: A Women's Poetry Anthology*. Natalie was awarded second place in the Poetry on the Lake short poem competition 2018 and the Oxford Brookes International Poetry Competition 2017. She lives in South East London, where she works as a secondary school teacher.

Heidi Williamson's *Electric Shadow* (Bloodaxe, 2011) was a Poetry Book Society Recommendation and shortlisted for the Seamus Heaney Centre for Poetry Prize. *The Print Museum (Bloodaxe,* 2016) won the East Anglian Book Award for Poetry. She teaches for The Poetry School and works with poets world-wide by Skype for the Poetry Society. She is Royal Literary Fund Fellow at the University of East Anglia. www.heidiwilliamsonpoet.com

Cliff Yates' poetry collections include *Henry's Clock*, which won both the Aldeburgh Prize and the Poetry Business Competition, *Frank Freeman's Dancing School* (Salt; KFS) and *Jam* (Smith/Doorstop). He wrote *Jumpstart Poetry in the Secondary School* during his time as Poetry Society poet-in-residence.

Tamar Yoseloff's fifth collection, *A Formula for Night: New and Selected Poems*, was published by Seren in 2015. She is also the author of *Formerly*, a chapbook incorporating photographs by Vici MacDonald (Hercules Editions, 2012) shortlisted for the Ted Hughes Award; two collaborative editions with the artist Linda Karshan; and a book with the artist Charlotte Harker. She is a London-based freelance tutor in creative writing and runs site-specific writing courses for galleries such as the Hayward, the RA and the National Gallery. She is currently a visiting guest lecturer at Newcastle University on the Newcastle / Poetry School MA course in Writing Poetry. Her sixth collection, *The Black Place*, is due from Seren in 2020.